I0413388

How 10 Kindle Covers Generate $3697.22 Every Day

–

Explode Your eBook Revenue using Simple Design Guidelines
by
Stijn B.

© 2013

The daily revenue "$ 3697.22" is estimated based on 10 high performing non-fiction books published in 2013.

TABLE OF CONTENTS

Introduction:
Judging Best-Selling eBooks by Their Covers

The eBook industry is big business, as witnessed by recent reports wherein Morgan Stanley estimated that Amazon would sell approximately $4.5 billion in Kindle e-readers and tablets in 2013 – a huge 26% jump in sales from the year prior.

The digital media revenue – which isn't just Kindle book sales, but also movies, games and other stuff – will account for $3.8 billion in sales in 2013. Amazon is notoriously tight-lipped about their sales numbers, but it's great to see the Morgan Stanley estimates in order to give us an idea of the sales successes.

It would be great to see a breakdown of how much of that $3.8 billion is directly attributable to Kindle book sales, but another report from 2013 gives us more clues. Scott Devitt, a top web e-commerce analyst from Morgan Stanley, told investors in a research note that Amazon sold a lot more eBooks than previously thought in 2012.

Devitt estimated that Amazon sold close to 383 million eBooks in 2012, a lot larger than the 252 million that was originally estimated that the online retailer sold.

Even using a conservative Kindle book price average of $3 in revenue received by Amazon per book (although many books are priced at 99 cents, lots of authors tend to price their books at $2.99 because that's the 70% royalty rate minimum), that would work out to $1.145 billion in Kindle book sales income for the retail giant in 2012.

Getting our piece of the Kindle book-selling pie by examining best-selling covers

Let's take one moment to wrap our heads around that number: $1.145 billion in Kindle book sales in 2012, according to estimates.

It's a number that's growing in spades. Morgan Stanley also estimated that the entire Kindle digital content business would create more revenue in 2014 than sales of the Kindle e-reader devices themselves — with that $3.8 billion jumping to an approximated $5.7 billion in revenue. And based on our rudimentary data suggesting that Kindle book sales make up 30% of those huge numbers, that means that Kindle eBook revenue could jump from $1.145 billion to $1.7 billion or more by 2014.

Now is the appointed time to get in on this Kindle book business. We've already watched Kindle eBooks begin outselling print editions of books, and now we're watching eBooks sales start to outstrip sales of the very devices people read them on – which was Jeff Bezos' plan from the beginning, when he reportedly sold Kindle devices at a loss, because he knew the real money was to be made via the digital content.

Seeing as though Morgan Stanley estimates that the whole world of Kindle moneymaking avenues – including its advertising revenue of $192 million – will make up 11% of Amazon's total revenue in 2013 and 23% of its operating profit, that's a good hint to us authors that the Kindle business is potentially here to stay.

So how do we grab our piece of the growing pie?

Good question. If you're an author interested in great, best-selling eBook covers – which you probably are if you're reading this – or a graphic design artist looking for tips on creating a best-selling cover, or a writer who wants to give his Photoshop guy some directions on knocking out a best-selling homerun, read on.

To follow are a plethora of real-life, best-selling eBook covers, and a study of what makes them great, along with tips on how you can emulate the look – and hopefully gain a bunch of book sales yourself!

Let's begin this journey, my friend…

Best-Selling eBook Cover #1: Breaking the Rules: Sometimes It's Not About the Cover at All

BOOK TITLE: *Choose Yourself*

AUTHOR: James Altucher

CURRENT SALES RANK ON AMAZON FOR KINDLE EDITION: #1,226

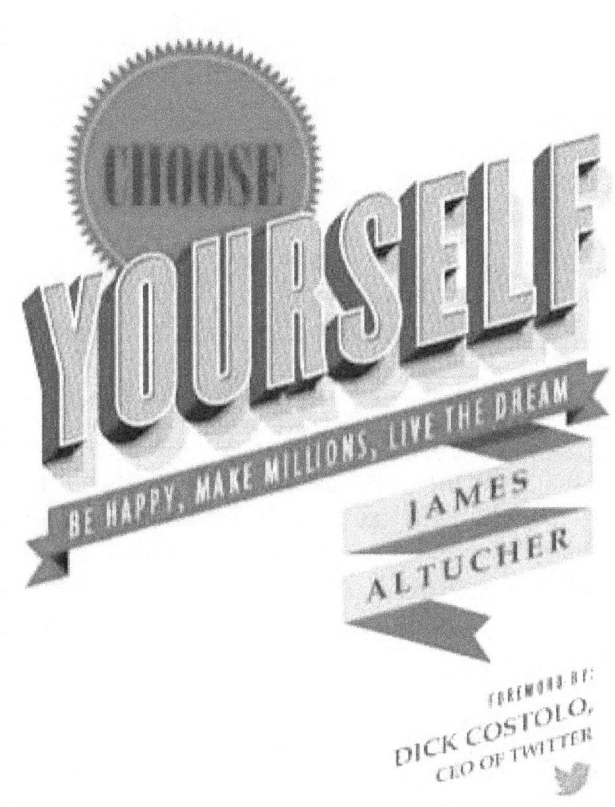

The book titled "Choose Yourself" by James Altucher, described as a "successful entrepreneur, chess master, investor and writer" on his Amazon author page, is the perfect beginning for this study about best-selling book covers.

The Positives:

Sure, the way the bold red appears in the shape of those "gold star" stickers stands out against the stark white background is appealing, along with the big and bold "YOURSELF" wording slanted upwards and to the right.

There's even something great about that ribbon and award-winning banner object in magenta that holds the "Be Happy, Make Millions, Live the Dream" subtitle and the lemon-lime colored author decoration.

And it can't hurt at all to have the Twitter bird logo in blue highlighting the fact that the forward of the book is written by Dick Costolo, CEO of Twitter.

How to Emulate This Look:

Normally, us authors are advised to stay away from white backgrounds, or to throw a grey border around them so they don't disappear into Amazon's white background, and that's been done with this book.

So go bold with a white background if you dare – I can see whereby it helps the impressive credentials "pop" on this book. But I'll tell you what, after soaking up one compelling essay on this guy's blog – a man who has gained 10 million readers since his blog launched in 2010 – Altucher could've probably simply thrown a photo of a hot dog on the cover of his 11th book and still have seen the winning sales numbers he's seeing now.

James' writing is amazing, and his author book video trailer for the "Choose Yourself" book on his Amazon page is even more compelling. My advice for attempting to duplicate his success is to write prose so compelling that people will buy your book no matter what the cover – but still keep it professional like he does.

And go with a white cover if you dare, especially if you've got impressive foreword writers with recognizable logos that need to "pop" out at readers.

Onward and upward, up the Amazon best-sellers list, that is. Let look at number two. (Tee hee hee.)

Best-Selling eBook Cover #2: The Book Cover Tips of a Best-Selling 'Regular' Writer

BOOK TITLE: *31 Days To A Clean And Organized Home: How To Organize, Clean, And Keep Your Home Spotless*

AUTHOR: BJ Knights

CURRENT SALES RANK ON AMAZON FOR KINDLE EDITION: #1,450

31 Days To A CLEAN AND ORGANIZED HOME

This next book sent me on quite the journey, and it was the perfect study of a "regular," not well known author enjoying a successful sales rank with a book cover that seems sort of average.

I mean, when you look at it, like I just did one more time, I realized that the author's name isn't even on the cover. The several hours of study into why this book is so successful – after all a "#1,450 Paid in Kindle Store" rank means that Knights could be selling close to 150 copies per day, according to some estimates that Kindle authors have devised.

Wow – with a current price of $2.99, which nets the author approximately $2.00 per copy sold, even if they were selling "only" 100 copies of the book per day, that's $200 daily income in Kindle royalty earnings!

Let's look a bit more into some of what I've uncovered about this book and its cover.

The Positives:

The book cover is actually very clean looking, with a great photo of a modernly designed living room – but as far as the text and font? Let's face it, we've seen better designs than this one.

The white text clashes with the tan background, or perhaps, fades into it – and the blue lettering looks crowded as the bottom of the letters hit the top of the couch. So it must be something more than the cover that's selling this book.

I found it when I paged down the Amazon product page and saw that this particular book has still found a way to manipulate their product description to have larger fonts and the all-important header tags, which may help its positioning. Just like days when books in the front of bookstores like Borders and Barnes & Noble probably got more sales due to their prominent positioning, this book might experience the same deal.

Folks who search for things on Amazon like "clean house" and "how to clean your house" are greeted with this book, which seems to offer a nice 89 pages of tips.

How to Emulate This Look:

This is a book cover that's easy to have – simply search for information about using Amazon's 'Cover Creator' module and you're good to go in creating this same type of look for your Kindle eBook cover. It looks like a simple stock image photo and standard types of fonts that lots of people could figure out how to do on their on – or something that would be a whiz for their book cover designer to replicate.

The larger question is how to get the description designed in a similar vein, something that's a moving target as Amazon strips out HTML code that authors try to sneak in their descriptions.

Some writers still find some ways to get it in there, constantly finding loopholes.

It's a clean cover, and one readily seen in a good position on Amazon for a number of search terms, so that helps account for its success.

Let's move on to the next book cover, a standout one.

Best-Selling eBook Cover #3: Bold, Red and Browse-Stopping

BOOK TITLE: *Gulp: Adventures on the Alimentary Canal*

AUTHOR: Mary Roach

CURRENT SALES RANK ON AMAZON FOR KINDLE EDITION: #1,253

Mary Roach

best-selling author of *Stiff*

Gulp.

ADVENTURES ON THE ALIMENTARY CANAL

One look at Mary Roach's "Gulp" book, and we can see why it's the kind of book that has stopped me in my Kindle browsing tracks before.

The Positives:

I mean, sham wow! This is a book cover that knows how to have an impact against a white background, and has me considering using something just as shocking to grab readers' eyeballs.

It doesn't hurt that Roach has been writing for years and appears to have several successful books, but no doubt it's that attention-grabbing cover with the big red (vector drawn?) mouth that's wide open, all white teeth and uvula exposed that has helped it get more exposure.

Her popular "Stiff" book goes for the shock value – in a good way – as well, with its close up shot of a man's feet and a toe tag dangling.

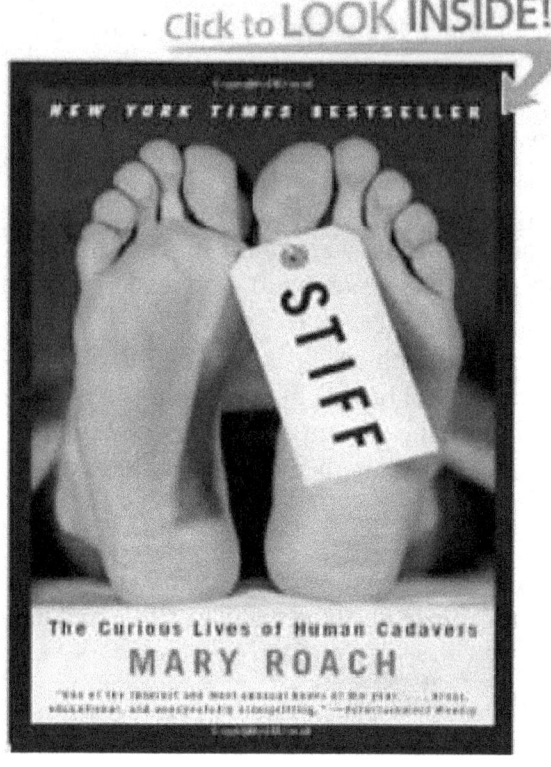

How to Emulate This Look:

There are several different ways to get this same kind of "shock effect" cover for your book. First off, you could always buy your own photo from a stock photo website like iStockPhoto.com, which has a boatload of amazing photographs – even the Oprah-touted best-seller "Wild" by Cheryl Strayed used a photo of a single boot on the cover of that book that is credited to the website.

Then you could use your own photo-editing software (or instruct your designer) to add the book's title and subtitle and author name in a similar manner, leaving the eyeball-grabbing photo as the star of the cover show.

Another way to attempt to get the same types of covers that authors like Roach use is to literally scout the book's copyright page for information about the cover image. For example, when I downloaded a free sample of "Wild," that's how I learned the boot book cover photo was from iStockPhoto.

Scanning the information on the copyright pages of various books you like may turn up their actual book designer – if a good Google search doesn't – and you might find out how to contact them directly to find out if they could create something similar for you.

Let's examine the phrase "cuteness counts" for our next cover.

Best-Selling eBook Cover #4: Babies and Puppies: Go For the Adorable and Irresistible

BOOK TITLE: *The Spaghetti Shots: How to Take Better Photos of Your Kids During Everyday Life*

AUTHOR: Courtney Westlake

CURRENT SALES RANK ON AMAZON FOR KINDLE EDITION: #61,953

the **Spaghetti** shots

how to take better photos
of your kids during everyday life

Courtney Westlake
award-winning children and family photographer

Even though Courtney Westlake's book, "The Spaghetti Shots," is
hovering around a sales rank of 60,000 as I write this (which
means it still sells a respectable 2 or 3 copies per day), I believe it
was a lot higher previously.

Not bad for a book that's priced at $4.99 right now, and one whose author doesn't even have an Amazon author page when you click her author name.

The Positives:

It's a smiling baby! Who can resist that cute smile of a beautiful baby with food all over his (or her?) face?

Doing a quick Google search, I see that Westlake is a popular photographer who has made it easy to decipher how folks can use their DSLR cameras in a lot easier way than reading their manuals.

And she made the best decision by choosing a cute close-up shot of a baby for the cover, with simple and cute fonts for the book title that looks like something designed pretty easily, perhaps in Photoshop – she is an award-winning photographer, after all, no doubt used to Photoshop.

How to Emulate This Look:

Get this same effect for your cover by either finding a dog to rival Boo, the cutest dog in the world who gained Internet fame by just looking so darned cute – like a stuffed animal or something, with that fluffy face – or use a charming and irresistible photo of a baby on your book cover.

When I took a trip to my local Hallmark store today, I loved looking at a book about Boo, and I even displayed the book more prominently when I put it back, just so other folks could see it and get a smile like I got.

Now that we've had a warm and fuzzy smile, let's turn serious with the next minimalist cover.

Best-Selling eBook Cover #5: Minimalism Rules

BOOK TITLE: *Her Best-Kept Secret: Why Women Drink-And How They Can Regain Control*

AUTHOR: Gabrielle Glaser

CURRENT SALES RANK ON AMAZON FOR KINDLE EDITION: #5,036

Her Best-Kept Secret

WHY WOMEN DRINK—AND HOW THEY
CAN REGAIN CONTROL

GABRIELLE GLASER

Our next book cover case study is titled "Her Best-Kept Secret:
Why Women Drink – And How They Can Regain Control," by
Gabrielle Glaser.

Methinks it's the compelling subject matter about women and the hidden-but-out-in-the-open alcoholism through the "acceptable" means of wine drinking that has resonated so much with readers, causing the success of this book. However, we can always cull a few tips from this beautiful cover to take to the bank with our own book covers.

The Positives:

Glaser's cover seems to have employed the minimalist design, with a single, half-full (yeah, I'm an optimist) glass of white wine that sits beautifully in front of the "secret" word, appearing to blur it a bit.

How to Emulate This Look:

First off, if you know Photoshop, it seems the "blur" feature would be in order in trying to create something similar to this effect. Or, have a knowledgeable cover designer (you might be able to find even cheap ones on Fiverr, Elance or oDesk) create this look for you – and it doesn't have to mimic the exact same wording-blurred-behind-a-glass look either.

The main point of this beautiful, somewhat haunting cover is the fact that the shadowy, muted tones of grey, coupled with the feminine purple bar across the front for the subtitle combine to make an impactful cover about and impacting subject – and in a very minimalistic sort of way.

Next up, we'll check out how putting your actual face on your eBook cover can make a huge difference in sales.

Best-Selling eBook Cover #6: I See Writing People – The Personal and Personality-Driven eBook Cover

BOOK TITLE: *Against all Grain: Delectable Paleo Recipes to Eat Well & Feel Great*

AUTHOR: Danielle Walker

CURRENT SALES RANK ON AMAZON FOR KINDLE EDITION: #1,900

Without having read it, I'm pretty impressed by this book simply by what I learned from its cover. Titled "Against all Grain: Delectable Paleo Recipes to Eat Well & Feel Great," I'm even more impressed by the words "written and photographed by" above the author Danielle Walker's name on the cover. Immediately, it tells me that this woman has class and know-how, because this is no shabby cover.

The Positives:

I don't know if that's Danielle's kitchen she's standing in, but the lighting is absolutely gorgeous, with all those windows giving a great and open and well lit feel to the cover.

It looks professionally photographed, which goes to show you that the modern-day DSLR cameras that a lot of people own can do a great job with cover photos. Heck, even the iPhone 5 has an amazing looking output to high-resolution photographs.

The cover also explains that she has included "over 150 gluten-free, grain-free & dairy-free recipes for daily life," something folks are obviously going gaga over with that excellent sales rank and glowing comments. (I would've written "more than 150…" but that's just the writer in me coming out.)

How to Emulate This Look:

Anyway, the thing I love about covers like this is that they are personality driven, featuring a real person on the cover so that readers know they are buying a book where they know who's talking to them, not some elusive, hidden person.

It helps that Danielle is really pretty – and it also helps that all that food – looks like pasta, bread and veggies – surrounding her is central to the topic at hand.

I know Paleo diet and recipe books are really hot right now, and this 623-page whopper of a book is obviously what readers are seeking.

If you want to copy this look for your book, it helps if your topic lends itself to putting a photo of yourself on the cover. And take a page from Danielle's book of cover creation: Find the best-looking locale where you can be photographed using the best equipment you can come up with, and stage it in a manner befitting your book topic.

That is all. Let's keep going and learning…by going backwards in time, when photos were all about the black, white and sepia tones.

Best-Selling eBook Cover #7: Go Old School: Crushing it With the Black and White and Sepia Tones

BOOK TITLE: *Life and Death in Assisted Living (Kindle Single)*

AUTHORS: A.C. Thompson & Jonathan Jones

CURRENT SALES RANK ON AMAZON FOR KINDLE EDITION: #4,040

One thing all of our book covers that we've examined thus far have had in common is color – and lots of it. After all, we live in an age when beautiful colors surround us every second of the day.

That's why it's good to "go old school" sometimes, flip the script and pull out those basic black and white or sepia tones that are now no longer the norm for our book covers, just to grab eyeballs that are used to being hypnotized by lots of colors.

The Positives:

This Kindle Single has obviously gotten a lot of attention simply by being in the Kindle Singles program on Amazon, a group of shorter books that are promoted more visibly.

However, it still takes a great eBook cover and subject matter to grab attention once we're there. In this instance, it was the compelling topic of assisted living, combined with an obviously aged photo of a pretty woman. A quick peek inside the book shows the cover photo is no doubt of a woman named Joan Boice.

Stephen Engelberg, Editor-in-Chief of ProPublica, starts off the Kindle Single with an old photo of his mom, Elaine Engelberg, just inside the book, which is also a sepia-toned wonder – and gorgeously titled to the side with white edges surrounding the photo.

How to Emulate This Look:

Seeing this book cover reminded me so much of the times that I've dug up old photos of my parents and grandparents and used my Wi-Fi all-in-one printer, scanner and fax machine to simply lay the photo on the glass bed, put the cover down and scan it into my computer, turning it into a jpg photo file.

That jpg (or png or whatever kind of file your scanner might create) can then be used as part of your book cover, either by you pulling it into a pre-prepared design program like Amazon's free Cover Creator, or by passing it on to your eBook designer.

My sister once wondered aloud to her friend, questioning how folks like me get old photos on the web – and the answer is by scanning them in! If you don't own a scanner at home, there are also places like FedEx Kinko's or other shops that can scan them in for you and provide you with a digital file.

The best thing to do is to search through any old photos you can get your hands on – especially if they are large in size and in good condition, to emulate the look of this cover. Your memoirs await!

Now let's take a look at a cover with no photos, but one that uses simple, large-letter boldness to get its point across.

Best-Selling eBook Cover #8: Big, Bold and Photo-less

BOOK TITLE: *The Business of Belief: How the World's Best Marketers, Designers, Salespeople, Coaches, Fundraisers, Educators, Entrepreneurs and Other Leaders Get Us to Believe*

AUTHOR: Tom Asacker

CURRENT SALES RANK ON AMAZON FOR KINDLE EDITION: #6,182

THE
BUSINESS
OF BELIEF

HOW THE WORLD'S BEST MARKETERS,
DESIGNERS, SALESPEOPLE, COACHES,
FUNDRAISERS, EDUCATORS, ENTREPRENEURS
AND OTHER LEADERS GET US TO BELIEVE

BELIEF

TOM ASACKER

While most of our book covers examined have featured some type of photo, this book has nary an image – and is replete with black, white and shades-of-gray big block text.

It's called, "The Business of Belief: How the World's Best Marketers, Designers, Salespeople, Coaches, Fundraisers, Educators, Entrepreneurs and Other Leaders Get Us to Believe," and I'll admit, while it's not my favorite design for a cover, since I tend to favor using pics, it is effective.

The Positives:

One of the best things about this cover is that it stopped me in my tracks due to its interesting dichotomy of words. "Business" and "belief" aren't always used so closely together, so that's what really drew my eye.

But the very fact that I could even read that book title via a small thumbnail image speaks volumes, and that's one big positive about this cover. Customers scrolling through websites that show a long list or page full of small images might do well to find this one easily because the lack of an image and the huge lettering makes for an easy read, even when it's so small.

How to Emulate This Look:

It may be a mistake to think that a "simple" looking cover like this can be done simply. Sure, it's not the complex photography that some covers have, with tons of crazy and wild Photoshop features. But this one might not be as easy as it looks, considering when you look at the letters closer, they appear to be carved into the book.

Folks like me who weren't Photoshop whizzes before I delved into the program more would do well to do what I did: a lot of Googling and YouTube tutorial watching to figure out how to do the things that the "Guided" tab on Photoshop Elements didn't teach me.

Or, if all that sounds like gobblygook to you, simply pass on this image of the same book cover you love to your designer, and tell him or her you want something just like it, and let them figure it all out.

And while they're figuring it all out, you might want to take a gander at our next cover, one that you might love even more that they could also imitate.

Best-Selling eBook Cover #9: How'd They Do That? The Double-Take Cover

BOOK TITLE: *Contagious: Why Things Catch On*

AUTHOR: Jonah Berger

CURRENT SALES RANK ON AMAZON FOR KINDLE EDITION: #6,607

Contagious

WHY THINGS CATCH ON

JONAH BERGER

"Jonah Berger knows more about what makes information 'go viral' than anyone in the world." –DANIEL GILBERT, Professor of Psychology, Harvard University and author of *Stumbling on Happiness*

The book cover for *Contagious: Why Things Catch On*, a book by Jonah Berger, is one that really draws consumers' eyes because at first you witness the normal dandelion with the seeds being blown away – a perfect metaphor for spreading something with a few seeds that can blossom into many other things.

But the "Wah?" moment comes when one notices the bottom of the dandelion, which is the bottom of a light bulb, not ugly roots.

The Positives:

The best thing about this cover isn't just its bold orange background – a perfect color to highlight the white of the dandelion and the brassy tone of the bulb bottom, but also that the dandelion in action matches perfectly with the title and theme of the book.

This is a no-brainer; your book's cover should match your book's theme and idea seamlessly. Also, just like this awesome cover accomplishes, having something unexpected on the cover can be a great addendum to complete the package.

When our eyes see something that takes our minds by surprise, we tend to do a double take, or a triple take, or a quadruple take – and all those second, third and fourth glances are helpful in bringing potential sales by encouraging readers to look further into our books. It helps to give them something beyond the great book cover, at that point, to look into once we've drawn their attention.

How to Emulate This Look:

Admittedly, a cover photo like this might be challenging to mimic for those of us who aren't masters at Photoshop. The good news is that plenty of stock photo websites like iStockPhoto and others come replete with excellent and amazing high-quality photos that offer unexpected images like these – you've just got to be willing to search them out, and pay a pretty penny for some of them if you fall in love with the photo.

I've paid approximately $148 in the past for a photo I loved that I found on iStockPhoto, so it's well worth the money if it brings you sales in perpetuity.

My advice for duplicating this cover look is to search out stock photography websites for an image that grabs your attention and matches your book's title and theme perfectly, and then either pass it on to your graphic designer or pull it into your favorite photo editing software and go to town.

Finally, let's move on to our last tip – hypnotizing folks with a hypnotic cover.

Best-Selling eBook Cover #10: Hypnotize Them With a Hypnotic eBook Cover

BOOK TITLE: *How to Get People to Do Stuff: Master the art and science of persuasion and motivation*

AUTHOR: Susan M. Weinschenk, Ph.D.

CURRENT SALES RANK ON AMAZON FOR KINDLE EDITION: #4,350

Okay, we're not going to literally hypnotize people, but in looking at that crazy visual, the circular optical illusion on the cover, can't you just hear the words, "You are getting very sleepy…" right about now?

The Positives:

We got a great title – I mean, "How To Get People to Do Stuff" just draws you in, what with that bold black and bolder red text breaking up the title and making "Do Stuff" scream out at you.

And using an optical illusion is pretty freaking brilliant. Once again, it falls right in line with the book's central theme and title.

Also, it helps that the author has a Ph.D., and displays that accomplishment after her name on her book, giving her the appearance of more authority.

How to Emulate This Look:

It may have taken me a few seconds to remember that this object is called an "optical illusion," but once I did, I Googled the term, and up popped lots of others – some of which can be ours for the taking, based on commercial copyright use laws.

Simply search for ones (or any photo, too, for that matter) that allows you to use it for your eBook cover, one that gives you express permission to use it so you won't have any worries later. Some artists allow a "creative agreement" or "exchange" whereby as long as you give them proper attribution in your book, they'll let you use their image or artwork for free.

The main point for this stunning optical illusion is that it's intriguing. There's a reason we pass these kinds of things along in emails – and in books, prior to the popularity of emails and Facebook and other social sharing sites. We like to see if other people can "find the old woman" or if they see a different image in the Rorschach test that we're viewing.

Be shocking, be bold, be classy – but find ways to get your eBook noticed with a stunning cover.

Wrapping it All Up in the End

Well, there we go.

We've examined ten best-seller eBook covers, and have picked apart each one to determine what specific tactics the authors or cover designers used to spark interest and increase sales.

Let's summarize what we've learned.

Here are 10 take-away tips for your eBook covers, based on the bestsellers:

#1 - Stay away from white backgrounds...

...unless you place a border around them to distinguish them from the white background of the website where it will be featured. Plus, if you've got high-profile logos or distinguished names that you want to "pop" out against the white, go full speed ahead with the alabaster.

#2 - Shock them...

...your readers, that is, with an unusual cover, something they don't expect, like Mary Roach's "Gulp" book, which displays the large rendering of an open mouth -- or her "Stiff" cover, with that close-up photo of a man's feet and a toe tag.

#3 - Show them how you look...

...by putting a photo of yourself on the cover, if it's a personality-driven book. Or if not, you can still use an image of a human being that relates to your book's theme, as long as it's an approved photo source.

#4 - Give them cuteness...

…with babies, bunnies, puppy dogs or anything else that makes them say, "Awww…." and hopefully click that "buy" button afterward.

#5 - Search for stock photos…

…that do the heavy lifting for you. Even if you do know your way around Photoshop, it can't hurt to peruse stock photo websites to find a stunning image that may be beyond anything you've thought of creating. If it's in your budget, it might be worth the buy if it brings enormous book sales in its wake.

#6 - Keep it clean and uncluttered…

…even if you have a ton of things to say. Save some of your words for the inside, or, if you go with big-time clutter on the cover, make it purposeful, unique and eye-catching.

#7 - Stick with your book's theme…

…for cohesiveness. I've seen some customer reviews for popular books that say things like "I almost didn't buy this because of the cover, but…"

Don't let your book gather comments like those. If it's a mysterious romance, select an appropriate, matching cover that reflects the tone of the writing. If it's humorous, go goofy, etc.

#8 - Use fonts large enough to read as a thumbnail photo…

…so that folks surfing through hundreds of small book images can still read your eBook's title from a mile away. (Okay, a few inches away.)

#9 - Try some shades of gray…

No, not those shades of gray. ;-)

I'm talking about digging out any black and white photos you can find, or sepia-toned gems laying around your home office or parents' house that you can steal. Er, borrow. Or even if they are photos of you decked out in your flair bottomed gauchos in the 1970s and they're in color, they still might make for a great book cover collage -- once you scan them or have them scanned for you and turned into photos.

Anything different than our normal HD world might stick out, in a great way.

#10 - Hypnotize them…

…not only with your mesmerizing prose, but perhaps an optical illusion on the cover – or go for a photo or word design that makes them look twice, thrice or more.

In the End

You really can judge a book by its cover – and even though some folks slap unprofessional or boring covers on their eBooks because of lack of time, money or knowledge, some of those books still survive based on their content – in spite of their bad covers.

Now that we know how to go about creating (or having created for us) some truly stunning covers, I hope you can move forward in getting a great new cover for your new eBook done.

Even if you already have a book out there and aren't in love with your cover, don't despair. That's the great thing about eBook covers – they're fluid, and the web allows you to change them up at the drop of a hat, unlike 10,000 print copy books sitting on shelves or in boxes.

So take what you've learned today and run with it…straight to your book cover designer or photo-editing software. And feel free to drop me a great comment about how this book helped improve your sales after you changed your book's cover.

Other resources (+ BONUS)

I am pleased to present you other material that you might have interest in.

1) Amazon Book "Create a Sales Page for Your Kindle Book"
Do you want your book description to look something similar to this?

Yes? Then, grab my other book right away at
http://www.amazon.com/Create-Kindle-Skyrocket-Central-ebook/dp/B00BAHKWX2. You'll learn some cool trick to make elements of your Amazon Book Page as (visually) appealing as possible and finally boost your sales.

Temporarily I also include a WYSIWYG editor.

2) Amazon Book "The Kindle Sales Booster System: The Hidden Secrets of the Amazon Ecosystem Exposed"
In this book, I'll share actionable content so you can start improving your book sales right away.
After reading this book you'll be able to:
- Decode the buying process of your audience
- Test different book variables (such as your title, your cover, etc.) with a laser-focused mindset
- Generate more sales

3) Publishing Software: PublishingTracker.com (interested in a FREE TRIAL ... read on)

Are you tired of manually tracking the performance of your Kindle Books? I can recommend you an automated solution. Using PublishingTracker you will have access to a u nique dashboard showing your rank and sales data over tim e. This gives you the power of doing better analysis r esulting in taking better decisions.

Take a look at the screenshot below and judge yours elf:

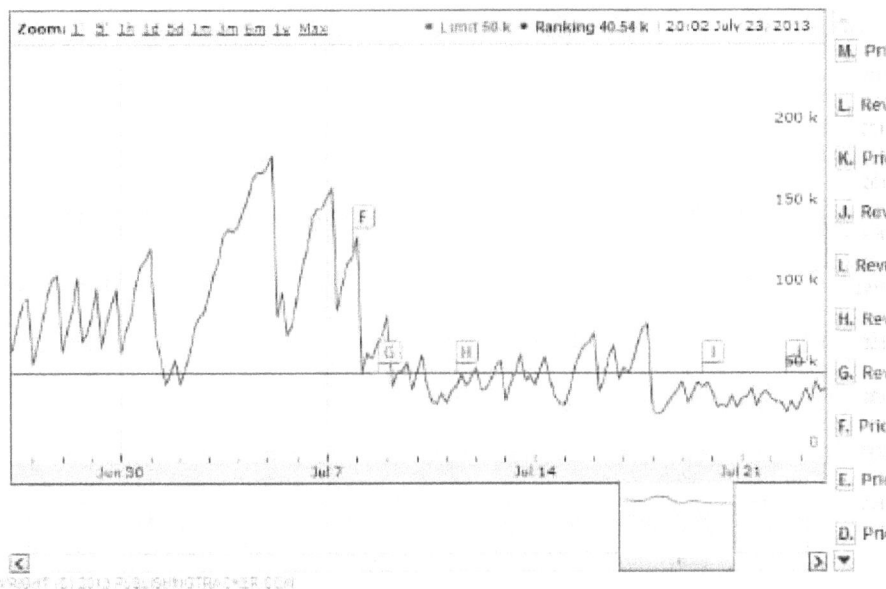

This screenshot shows you the performance of a Kind le Book over time together with some events.

Date	Views (Unique)	Amazon Email	Amazon Similar	Amazon Keywords	Amazon Other
08/10/13	15 (13)	2	2	author central (5) ; author page (1) ; amazon sales pages (1) ; create sales page (1) ; author central sign in (1)	0
08/09/13	14 (14)	4	1	create a sales page for your book (1) ; create a sales page for your kindle book (1) ; author central log in (1)	3
08/08/13	21 (20)	4	0	create a sales page for your kindle (1) ; author central (1) ; author page (1) ; Book marketing (1)	5
08/07/13	18 (18)	0	0	author central (1) ; amazon author central (1) ; books on sale on (1) ; author central log in (1) ; author central sign in (2) ; author page (1) ; sales page (1)	5

This screenshot shows you which keywords people use to find one of your Kindle Books.

Thank You

I really like to say thank you for purchasing my book. It really means a lot you picked this book out of hundreds of other books out there.

If you liked what you've read then I need your help!
Please take a moment to leave a review for this book on Amazon:
http://www.amazon.com/dp/B00EVA5J38.
Your valuable feedback means a lot and will keep giving me a drive to publish more inspiring books.

Before you go

I want to offer you a FREE 30 DAY PublishingTracker trial account as my gift to you.
Just send me an email (stijn@publishingtracker.com) and I'll set you up an account.

Take care!

Stijn

Don't hesitate contacting me at stijn@publishingtracker.com if you have any question.